100
H

BROWS

D0742653

X   c.3
551.2
Asimov
    How did we   t
quakes.

F PUBLIC
ON
HOOLS
OUNTY

ADIA, CALIFORNIA

HOW DID WE FIND OUT
ABOUT EARTHQUAKES

HOW DID WE FIND OUT . . . SERIES
Each of the books in this series on the history of science
emphasizes the process of discovery.

How Did We Find Out . . . ?
Books by Isaac Asimov

HOW DID WE FIND OUT
THE EARTH IS ROUND?

HOW DID WE FIND OUT ABOUT
ELECTRICITY?

HOW DID WE FIND OUT ABOUT
NUMBERS?

HOW DID WE FIND OUT ABOUT
DINOSAURS?

HOW DID WE FIND OUT ABOUT
GERMS?

HOW DID WE FIND OUT ABOUT
VITAMINS?

HOW DID WE FIND OUT ABOUT
COMETS?

HOW DID WE FIND OUT ABOUT
ENERGY?

HOW DID WE FIND OUT ABOUT
ATOMS?

HOW DID WE FIND OUT ABOUT
NUCLEAR POWER?

HOW DID WE FIND OUT ABOUT
OUTER SPACE?

HOW DID WE FIND OUT ABOUT
EARTHQUAKES?

HOW DID WE FIND OUT

ABOUT EARTHQUAKES?

Isaac Asimov

Illustrated by David Wool

DEPARTMENT OF PUBLIC INSTRUCTION ELEMENTARY SCHOOLS ARCADIA UNIFIED SCHOOL DISTRICT LOS ANGELES COUNTY ARCADIA, CALIFORNIA

X
551.2
A   c. 3

TITLE IV

WALKER AND COMPANY
New York

Library of Congress Cataloging in Publication Data

Asimov, Isaac, 1920–
    How did we find out about earthquakes?

    (How did we find out . . . books)
    Includes index.
    SUMMARY: Traces the history of man's study of earth-
quakes, discusses what is currently known about these
tremors, and explores the possibility of their prevention.
    1. Earthquakes—Juvenile literature. [1. Earth-
quakes] I. Title.
QE534.2.A84   551.2'2   78-4098
ISBN 0-8027-6305-7
ISBN 0-8027-6306-5 lib. bdg.

Text Copyright © 1978 by Isaac Asimov
Illustrations Copyright © 1978 by David Wool

All rights reserved. No part of this book may
be reproduced or transmitted in any form or by
any means, electronic or mechanical, including
photocopying, recording, or by any information
storage and retrieval system, without permission
in writing from the Publisher.

First published in the United States of America
in 1978 by the Walker Publishing Company, Inc.

Published simultaneously in Canada by Fitzhenry &
Whiteside, Limited, Toronto.

TRADE ISBN: 0-8027-6305-7
REINF. ISBN: 0-8027-6306-5

Library of Congress Catalog Card Number: 77-78984

Printed in the United States of America.

10 9 8 7 6 5 4 3 2 1

To Howard Gorfinkel, M.D.

Contents

HOW DID WE FIND OUT
ABOUT EARTHQUAKES

1 Gods and Air

IF THERE is anything that seems solid and steady, it is the earth beneath us. We move; the wind blows; the sea has waves and tides; but the ground we stand on always remains in place, firm and steady.

Always?

Every once in a while in some part of the world or another the ground suddenly rumbles and shakes. Cracks appear in the ground. Water pipes, gas pipes, and power lines break. Buildings fall down and people are trapped and killed inside. Then everything settles down and is quiet again.

The earth has "quaked" (which means "shaken" or "shivered"), and we call the event an *earthquake*.

Sometimes an earthquake may take place under the ocean. The water shakes above it, and a long wave is produced. That wave travels toward land.

Sometimes the wave enters a harbor where a stretch of sea narrows. The wave piles into the narrowing harbor and gets higher and higher. By the time it reaches land, it may be a tall tower of moving water that tumbles ashore, drowning everyone who didn't reach high ground.

11

tsunami

Such a tall wave is often called a *tidal wave*, but it has nothing to do with tides. A better name has been taken from the Japanese. It is now called a *tsunami* (tsoo-NAH-mee), which means "harbor wave."

An earthquake or a tsunami might only last five minutes. It comes suddenly, however, and without warning, and it could happen in places where there are many people. Hundreds of thousands of people might die in those five minutes. No other kind of natural disaster kills so many people in so short a time.

In a way, then, people have always known about earthquakes. They have been happening as long as the earth has existed, and anyone who has lived through an earthquake or tsunami never forgets it.

What people did not know was the cause of the earthquakes.

In ancient times people thought earthquakes might be the result of the anger of some god. After all, what else could be strong enough to shake the ground? The Greeks thought Poseidon (poh-SY-don), the god of the sea, was the god of earthquakes, too. When he furiously shook his trident (a three-pointed spear), the sea stormed and the earth quaked. The Greeks called him Poseidon, Earth-shaker.

Some ancient people thought the world had to be held up by something or it would fall. Often they imagined it was held up by some giant god or by some giant animals. Every once in a while, they supposed, the earth bearer would get weary and shift his burden from one shoulder to another. When he did that, there would be an earthquake.

Poseidon

Some people thought it was a fire god who was responsible. Earthquakes often took place in regions where volcanoes existed. Volcanoes spewed out smoke, flame, and floods of melted rock, so people had good reason for thinking there must be fire underneath.

The Hawaiians thought that the fire goddess, Pele (PAY-luh), lived in the giant volcano on their island. Everytime she grew angry and stamped her feet, she caused an earthquake.

Pele

14

The Greeks thought that a group of rebellious giants who were defeated by the gods were imprisoned under the volcanoes. Whenever they stirred and tried to break their chains, the earth shook.

The first person we know of who tried to think up a cause for earthquakes that did not involve gods was a Greek philosopher, Aristotle (AR-is-TOT-ul), who lived from 384 B.C. to 322 B.C.

Aristotle believed that every kind of substance had its own natural place. The solid earth was at the bottom and the water of the ocean lay above it, while the air was above both land and sea.

If any substance were trapped in an unnatural place, it would try to return to its natural place. Thus any solid matter that belongs to the earth falls to earth at once if it is taken up into the air and released.

In the same way, if any air were trapped underground, it should move upward to get to where air belongs. Aristotle thought that there were large quantities of air in holes and caves underground. When this air blew about in an attempt to get upward, earthquakes resulted.

There was no evidence for this, but it seemed to make sense at the time. There was no better idea for many centuries.

2 Detecting the Waves

EARTHQUAKES continued to take place and kill people, and there was nothing anyone could do about it.

On January 24, 1556, an earthquake struck in the province of Shensi in China and is supposed to have killed 830,000 people. That is still the worst record for earthquake deaths. On December 30, 1703, an earthquake killed 200,000 people in Tokyo, Japan, and on October 11, 1737, another killed 300,000 in Calcutta, India.

In those days, though, the people of western Europe, where science was developing, paid little attention to events that were far away.

Then, on November 1, 1755, something took place right in western Europe. On that day, an earthquake shook the city of Lisbon, the capital of Portugal, and the area in the ocean nearby.

Nearly every house in the city was knocked down, trapping thousands of people in the ruins. Then a

Engravings showing Lisbon before and after the earthquake of 1755 (Camera Municipal de Lisboa)

tsunami swept into the harbor. A wave, fifty feet high, crashed over the ruins. Two more shocks followed and fires broke out. When the sea moved back and the ground steadied itself, 60,000 people were dead.

The earthquake was worst in Lisbon, but there was damage elsewhere in Portugal. In Morocco, south across the Strait of Gibraltar, many thousands of people were also killed. Some shaking could be felt over millions of square miles, all over southern Europe and as far north as Scotland.

Everyone in Europe thought about earthquakes after that time, and Aristotle's theory of air under the ground wasn't good enough. Scientists knew a little more about energy and about the structure of the earth in the 1700s, and they were sure that there wasn't much air under the ground. Even if there were, the air wouldn't have enough energy to cause earthquakes.

One of the scientists who studied the structure of the earth was an Englishman named John Michell (1724–1793). He had noticed, as others had, that when one dug into the earth, the exposed rocks existed in layers called *strata* (STRAY-tuh). Sometimes these layers were flat, but sometimes they were tilted or curved. It was as though something had twisted the very structure of the earth.

Rock strata

In 1760 Michell said that the twisting of the strata might cause layers of rock to grind against one another, setting up a series of waves that would spread out from the place where the grinding happened. Those waves would be the earthquake.

Michell was the first to say that an earthquake could take place under the sea and set up a tsunami. He said that that was what had happened to Lisbon.

He also said that if the time the earthquake was felt in different places was noted, people would get an idea of how fast the waves traveled. They could calculate backward and figure out where the waves started.

That start, the point on the earth's surface over the place where the rocks ground together, is the *epicenter* (EP-ee-SEN-ter) of the earthquake.

Michell noticed, as many ancients did, that many earthquakes took place in regions where volcanoes existed, and he knew that heat is an important form of energy.* He thought that the heat of volcanoes supplied the energy to produce earthquakes. There might be underground water (this would be much more likely than underground air), which would be heated and turned into steam by volcanic heat. The expanding steam would move the rocks and cause an earthquake.

This was an improvement on Aristotle's idea. But how could scientists find out more about earthquakes? Could the earthquake waves that Michell talked about be studied?

*See *How Did We Find Out About Energy* (New York: Walker, 1975).

Naturally, one wouldn't want to study a large earthquake right where it was happening. Anyone studying earthquakes in Lisbon on November 1, 1755, was very likely to have been dead five minutes after he started the study.

The earthquake waves weaken as they spread outward, and even a giant earthquake can be studied safely if a scientist is a hundred miles away.

Then, too, for every large and deadly earthquake, there are many of medium size, which just rattle the windows and dishes. There are very many more that are so small they can hardly be felt.

Is there any way of detecting the little shivers set up by small earthquakes or by large earthquakes far away?

It wasn't till 1855, a hundred years after the great Lisbon earthquake, that the first such device was built. The inventor was an Italian scientist, Luigi Palmieri (pahl-MYEH-ree) (1807–1896).

Palmieri's invention consisted of a horizontal tube turned up at each end and partly filled with mercury. Whenever the ground shook, the mercury moved from side to side. The stronger the shake, the greater the movement and the more the mercury shifted into the turned-up-ends, first on one side and then on the other.

Palmieri placed small iron floats on the mercury in each upturned end, and he placed a marked-off rule behind each end. He could see how high the iron floats lifted as the mercury moved.

This was the first *seismometer* (size-MOM-ih-ter), from Greek words meaning "to measure earthquakes."

DEPARTMENT OF PUBLIC INSTRUCTION ELEMENTARY SCHOOLS LOS ANGELES COUNTY ARCADIA UNIFIED SCHOOL DISTRICT ARCADIA, CALIFORNIA

21

Palmieri's seismometer wasn't really much good. Almost anything could produce small shaking in the instrument, so it was hard to tell whether the seismometer was detecting a distant earthquake or a cart rumbling along a road nearby.

A better device was invented in 1880 by an English scientist named John Milne (1850–1913).

In 1875 he went to Tokyo, Japan, to teach geology and mining at the Imperial College of Engineering. That gave him an excellent chance to study earthquakes, which are very common in Japan. In 1880 he finally constructed a device that made it possible to study earthquakes in detail.

Here's how it works:

Imagine a heavy cylinder attached by a horizontal metal rod to a vertical support. A wire extends from the cylinder to the top of the support.

Where the horizontal metal rod connects to the vertical support there is a movable joint so that the cylinder can swing freely.

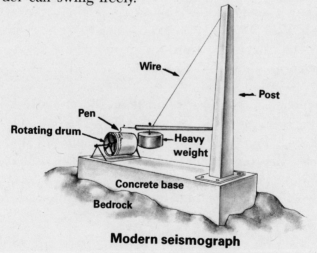

Modern seismograph

The wire that attaches the cylinder to the top of the support keeps the cylinder from moving down, and gravity keeps it from moving up. Therefore, the only way the cylinder can move is left and right in a horizontal line. If the instrument is protected from jolts and other disturbances, the cylinder doesn't move right or left either. It just remains steady.

The support is attached to a concrete block that is anchored to bedrock, the solid rock underneath the soil.

Now suppose there is an earthquake. The bedrock shakes back and forth, and the support shakes back and forth with it. If the cylinder were attached firmly to the support, it would shake back and forth also. It doesn't though. It is attached by a joint that lets it remain loose, While the bedrock and the support shake, the cylinder remains in one place.

Next imagine a pen attached to the cylinder, a pen that just touches a piece of paper wrapped about another cylinder that slowly rotates. This second cylinder, a *rotating drum*, is also attached to the concrete block that is attached to bedrock.

If the earth is perfectly steady, then, as the drum rotates, the pen marks out a straight line on the turning paper. If an earthquake strikes and the bedrock shakes, the rotating drum shakes back and forth, too. The pen attached to the cylinder (which doesn't move) therefore marks out a wavy line back and forth. The harder the ground and the rotating drum shake back and forth, the bigger the sweep of the ink mark.

This device is called a *seismograph* (SIZE-moh-graf), from Greek words meaning "earthquake writing," because the existence and strength of an earthquake is marked out in writing by the pen.

Of course, a pen making marks on paper moves with a certain amount of friction, or rubbing. That makes it harder to detect very tiny earth movements.

Nowadays, therefore, instead of ordinary paper, there is photographic paper that is sensitive to light on the rotating drums and there is a little mirror on the cylinder. A thin beam of light is reflected from the mirror onto the photographic paper. A line can be developed in that way that is more likely to reveal tiny waves than is one produced by pen and ink.

Then, too, the cylinder, nowadays, is surrounded by metal coils in which there are electric currents. These currents change as the earth moves, and that magnifies the shifts, back and forth, of the current of light and makes the device more sensitive.

Milne set up a number of seismographs in various places in Japan, and some elsewhere, too. By 1900 he had thirteen of them operating. Nowadays, there are many hundreds of seismographs on every continent of the world, even in Antarctica.

3 The Inside of the Earth

ONCE SCIENTISTS started studying seismograph records carefully, they found that there were different kinds of earthquake waves. Some waved left and right, some waved backward and forward. Some traveled along the surface of the earth, and some traveled through the body of the earth.

The different kinds of waves traveled at different speeds. That meant that different kinds of waves spreading outward from an earthquake with a distant epicenter arrived at the seismograph at different times. Scientists would time the appearance of one kind of wave, then of the next kind, then of the next kind, and so on.

The farther the epicenter, the greater the time lag between one kind of wave and the next. From the amount of time lag someone at a seismograph could tell how far off the epicenter of the earthquake was.

He couldn't tell from which direction the waves were coming, though. If the epicenter were five hundred miles away, it could be on any point on a

Berkeley

St. Louis

Cambridge

Epicenter

circle marked out five hundred miles from the seismograph in every direction.

Suppose, though, there are three seismographs in
different places, far apart from each other. The epicenter is five hundred miles from the first, seven
hundred miles from the second, and one thousand
miles from the third. If you draw circles of the proper
size on the map with each seismograph at the center of
one of the circles, the three circles will all cross at one
point. That point is the epicenter.

People at one seismograph can easily contact all other seismographs by radio these days. For that reason, any earthquake anywhere in the world is detected very quickly on a number of seismographs, and scientists can tell exactly where the epicenter is almost at once.

From the amount of the swing of the line back and forth, a seismograph shows how strong the waves are at that place. Once you know the distance that place is from the epicenter, you can calculate how strong the waves are at the epicenter and therefore how powerful an earthquake is.

In 1935 the American scientist Charles Francis Richter (1900–   ) worked out a way of expressing the power of earthquakes by means of a series of numbers from 1 up. This is called the *Richter scale.*

An earthquake that is 1 on the Richter scale has the amount of power in the explosion of six ounces of TNT. This creates waves so small it can only be detected by a seismograph. An earthquake that is 2 on the Richter scale is about thirty-one times as powerful. Each time you move up one number, the earthquake is thirty-one times more powerful than the number below.

CLASS	a	b	c	d	e
magnitude	7¾-8½	7.0-7.7	6-6.69	5.3-5.9	below 5.3
distance recorded	world wide		up to 90° (10,000 km.)	up to 45° (5,000 km.)	not beyond 10°

Richter scale

By the time you reach 9 on the Richter scale, the power of an earthquake is equal to that of the explosion of two-hundred million tons of TNT.

However, no earthquake has ever been measured that has quite reached 9 on the Richter scale. Even 8, though, is pretty tremendous. In 1906 the earthquake that destroyed San Francisco is supposed to have been about 8.25 on the Richter scale. In 1964 there was a very strong earthquake in Anchorage, Alaska, that registered 8.5, and some earthquakes have been estimated as 8.9.

San Francisco Earthquake 1906

Naturally, these giant earthquakes are very rare. There might be about a million earthquakes here and there on the earth every year, but most are small. Only one earthquake a year, on the average, is 8 or more on the Richter scale. Some years are quakier than average, of course. In 1906, there were seven earthquakes that were probably 8 or better.

A very powerful earthquake may just happen to take place where there are very few people and may do much less damage than a weaker earthquake that hits a crowded city. Again, a city with strong buildings may suffer less than one with flimsy structures. You can't go entirely by the Richter scale in judging how dangerous an earthquake is or whether it is a "killer" or not.

The *surface waves* set up by earthquakes, those waves that travel along the outside skin of the earth, give us useful information. The *body waves*, which travel from a point on the earth's surface right through the body of the earth to another point on the surface, are even more interesting.

The body waves were the first things that were ever found to travel deep into the earth and then back to the surface. Perhaps they could give us information about the deep interior of the earth, information we could get in no other way.

In 1909 a scientist started work on this problem. He was born in Austria-Hungary, in a place now in Yugoslavia. His name was Andrija Mohorovicic (moh-ho-ro-VEE-cheech) (1857–1936).

He showed that body waves that don't go very deep into the earth move more slowly than surface waves.

The deeper the body waves go, though, the faster they move. If they go deep enough they may be as fast as surface waves or even faster.

The reason for this is that rocks that are deep inside the earth are pressed together by the weight of the rocks above. A particular volume of deep rock weighs more than the same volume of rock on the surface. The deep rock is "more dense" than the surface rock. The deeper the rock, the greater the density.

Waves generally travel more rapidly through dense material than through less dense material of the same sort.

Mohorovicic studied the results shown by seismographs farther and farther from an epicenter. He saw that at the closer seismographs the body waves arrived after the surface waves. But to reach the seismographs farther and farther from the epicenter, the body waves penetrated deeper and deeper into the earth, moving faster and faster. Finally, if the seismograph was far enough away from the epicenter, the body waves actually arrived ahead of the surface waves.

From the speed of the body waves scientists could calculate what the density of the rocks must be at different distances under the earth's surface. The density increased smoothly or continuously as the depth grew greater and greater.

At certain distances from the epicenter, though, the body waves arrived unexpectedly quickly. They had penetrated to a depth where their speed suddenly increased more than it should have.

It seemed to Mohorovicic that at a certain depth below the earth's surface, there was a sudden sharp increase in density as though the waves had entered a new kind of rock, a kind considerably denser than the rock just above it.

A sudden change in properties is called a *discontinuity*. In honor of the discoverer, this particular discontinuity is called the *Mohorovicic discontinuity*.

The Mohorovicic discontinuity can be found all around the earth and is anywhere from three to forty miles under the surface. It is deeper under the continents than under the oceans.

The portion of the earth above the Mohorovicic discontinuity is the *crust*. The portion underneath it is the *mantle*. We know about the mantle only through earthquake waves, but from those we can figure out what the rocks in the mantle must be like. Someday, perhaps, scientists will be able to drill right through the crust and bring up rock from the mantle in order to study it.

A German scientist, Beno Gutenberg (1889-1960), who later came to the United States and became an American citizen, discovered something new.

In 1913 Gutenberg studied earthquake waves that go right through the earth, passing near its very center. He was able to show that when such waves reach a certain depth, they can change speeds and even direction very sharply. There is another discontinuity about eighteen hundred miles under the earth's surface. This is called the *Gutenberg discontinuity*.

The mantle reaches from the Mohorovicic discontinuity down to the Gutenberg discontinuity. From the Gutenberg discontinuity down to the very center of the earth is the *core*.

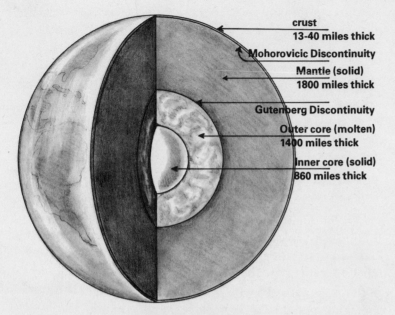

crust
13-40 miles thick
Mohorovicic Discontinuity
Mantle **(solid)**
1800 miles thick

Gutenberg Discontinuity

Outer core (molten)
1400 miles thick

Inner core (solid)
860 miles thick

Earth's Interior

This meant that the earth has a structure that resembles the structure of an egg in some ways. The central core is like the yolk of the egg. This is surrounded by the mantle, which is like the white of the egg. And all of it is surrounded by the crust, which is like the shell of the egg.

The deeper we go into the earth, the hotter it gets. By the time we get to the Gutenberg discontinuity, the temperature is about 5000° F. The mantle is solid, but it is very hot.

The core is even hotter.

There are two kinds of body waves. One kind moves forward and backward and is called a *longitudinal wave*. The other moves left and right and is called a *transverse wave*.

When a longitudinal wave reaches the Guten discontinuity, it changes direction but keeps on go A transverse wave, however, stops at the Guten discontinuity and goes no farther.

Scientists knew that a longtitudinal wave can through a liquid but a transverse wave cannot.

They concluded, therefore, that earth's core m liquid since it will not transmit a transverse Since the core is liquid and very dense, it m metal instead of rock. The most common dens is iron, so most scientists think that the earth's a mass of liquid iron, together with a small qu nickel, an element very similar to iron.

So earthquakes aren't all bad. At least th given us information about the inside of th right down to the center. It is information never have been able to get any other way.

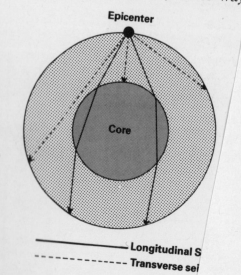

Epicenter

Core

————————— **Longitudinal S**
- - - - - - - - - - **Transverse se**

4 Shrinking and Drifting

San Andreas Fault

USING EARTHQUAKES to get information about the inside of the earth still doesn't tell us what causes them.

People began to notice that earthquakes took place near where there seemed to be long cracks in the rock. There would be long straight lines where the ground on one side didn't seem to match the ground on the other exactly. These lines are called *faults*.

The most famous one is the *San Andreas fault* (san-AN-dray-us) in western California. It was along this fault that an earthquake destroyed San Francisco in 1906.

After an earthquake has taken place, one side of the fault shifts. It may move forward as much as ten or twenty feet, or upward by that amount, or both. The other side moves backward or downward or both ways.

This made it look as though Michell was certainly right. The rock on one side of the fault moved relative to the rock on the other side, and the rubbing of the two sides set up the waves and the trembling. If there is enough movement and enough rubbing, the result would be a giant earthquake.

But what causes the movement?

Once scientists realized how hot the inside of the earth was, the possibility arose that the earth was cooling down. Perhaps it was *very* hot when it was first formed and has been cooling down ever since. As the earth cooled, it would shrink and its crust might wrinkle, forming mountains. That would be a very slow process, but every once in a while, as the mountains formed, one mass of rock would rub against another, setting off an earthquake.

This theory didn't work out. In the 1890s scientists discovered that atoms of certain heavy elements, such as uranium and thorium, are breaking down little by little. Each breakdown gives off a little heat.* Not much heat is given off when one atom breaks down, but every second, billions and billions of atoms are breaking down all over the earth. The heat all those atoms give off keeps the inside of the earth from cooling down. This means the earth is not shrinking and

---

*See *How Did We Find Out About Nuclear Power* (New York: Walker, 1976).

wrinkling and that this is not the way earthquakes are caused.

Another theory got started because of the shape of the continents.

If you will look at a map of the world, you will see that the shape of the eastern coast of South America resembles the shape of the western coast of Africa. If you imagine moving those two continents together, they would almost fit like a jigsaw puzzle.

This was noticed as long ago as 1620 by the English scholar Francis Bacon (1561–1626).

Could it be that once South America and Africa were a single body of land? Could it be that this single body split somehow and the two halves drifted apart?

This is exactly what a German scientist, Alfred Lothar Wegener (VAY-guh-ner) (1880–1930), thought.

Alfred Wegener

In 1912 he suggested that many millions of years ago, all the continents existed as a single large piece of land. He called that one large piece *Pangaea* (pan-JEE-uh), from Greek words meaning "all earth."

Pangaea split up, he thought, and the separate continents slowly drifted apart.

Wegener pointed out that the continents are made up mostly of a kind of rock called *granite* (GRAN-it). The ocean bottom is made up mostly of a denser kind of rock called *basalt* (buh-SAWLT), which also lies under the granite of the continents.

Objects can float on denser material, as wood floats on water. Wegener said that the continents are lumps of granite that float on a basalt layer that encompasses the whole world. Naturally the continents floated apart from one another only very slowly, less than an inch a year, because basalt is a lot stiffer than water is.

Wegener thought that the American continents were still drifting westward. The westernmost part, he thought, pushed slowly through the basalt, wrinkling and crumpling into mountain ranges—the Rockies in North America and the Andes in South America.

Naturally, this wrinkling and crumpling would cause masses of rock to rub against each other, and that would set off earthquakes.

Wegener's idea of *continental drift* was interesting. As time went on, scientists discovered a number of things that might be explained by it. The nature of the rocks in different continents indicated that those different continents might have once fitted together. The kinds of plants and animals that existed millions of

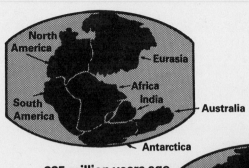

North America
Eurasia
Africa
India
South America
Australia
Antarctica

225 million years ago

135 million years ago

70 million years ago

Present

years ago made it seem that it must have been easy to get from one continent to another once, even though those same continents are far apart now.

Just the same, Wegener's theory was not accepted. The trouble was that granite continents would not drift on the basalt underneath. They wouldn't even move a fraction of an inch a year. The basalt is so stiff and hard that the continents would stay in one place and never budge.

For about fifty years after Wegener first talked about continental drift, therefore, scientists paid very little attention to the notion.

5 The Moving Plates

THE BIG CLUE came from the ocean bottom.

Until the 1900s, no one knew what the ocean bottom was like. You couldn't see it through the water, and nobody could penetrate more than a few yards underwater to look.

The most that could be done was to put a weight at the end of a long chain and drop it over the side of a ship. The chain would be lowered until it hit bottom, and that way the depth of the ocean at that point could be measured. It was not easy to do, people ended up with just a few depth measurements here and there.

A number of depths were measured in the Atlantic Ocean in the 1850s, for instance. At that time, people were trying to put a cable all the way across the bottom of the ocean so that telegraph messages could be sent back and forth between North America and Europe.

The depths that were measured then made it seem that the Atlantic Ocean wasn't as deep in the middle as it was on either side. There seemed to be high ground, or a "plateau," in the middle, which was named Telegraph Plateau.

During World War I (1914–1918) the French scientist Paul Langevin (lanzh-VAN) (1872–1946) worked out a way of producing certain kinds of sound waves that could streak through water, strike solid objects, and bounce back. If you could detect this echo and measure the time it took the sound waves to strike the object and return from a particular direction, you could tell the distance of the object in that direction.

Langevin meant his invention to be used to detect enemy submarines, but the war ended before he was finished. After the war the same invention was used to bounce the sound waves off the ocean bottom (sonar). In this way the ocean depth could be easily determined in many places very quickly.

In 1922 a German vessel, the *Meteor*, carrying the sound wave device, began to measure depths in the Atlantic Ocean.

The scientists discovered that the high ground in the middle of the Atlantic is not a flat plateau but is very uneven. In fact, by 1925 they were able to show that there is a huge mountain range curving down the mid-Atlantic from the Arctic to the Antarctic.

In later years it was discovered that the mountain range isn't in the Atlantic only. It can be traced around the southern end of Africa and up the middle of the Indian Ocean. It moves into the Pacific Ocean as well.

It came to be called the *Mid-Oceanic Range*.

increase in density as though the waves had entered a new kind of rock, a kind considerably denser than the rock just above it.

A sudden change in properties is called a *discontinuity*. In honor of the discoverer, this particular discontinuity is called the *Mohorovicic discontinuity*.

The Mohorovicic discontinuity can be found all around the earth and is anywhere from three to forty miles under the surface. It is deeper under the continents than under the oceans.

The portion of the earth above the Mohorovicic discontinuity is the *crust*. The portion underneath it is the *mantle*. We know about the mantle only through earthquake waves, but from those we can figure out what the rocks in the mantle must be like. Someday, perhaps, scientists will be able to drill right through the crust and bring up rock from the mantle in order to study it.

A German scientist, Beno Gutenberg (1889-1960), who later came to the United States and became an American citizen, discovered something new.

In 1913 Gutenberg studied earthquake waves that go right through the earth, passing near its very center. He was able to show that when such waves reach a certain depth, they can change speeds and even direction very sharply. There is another discontinuity about eighteen hundred miles under the earth's surface. This is called the *Gutenberg discontinuity*.

The mantle reaches from the Mohorovicic discontinuity down to the Gutenberg discontinuity. From the Gutenberg discontinuity down to the very center of the earth is the *core*.

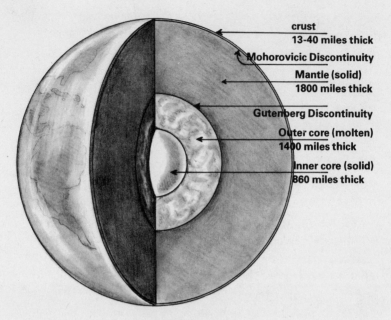

crust
13-40 miles thick
Mohorovicic Discontinuity
Mantle (solid)
1800 miles thick
Gutenberg Discontinuity
Outer core (molten)
1400 miles thick
Inner core (solid)
860 miles thick

Earth's Interior

This meant that the earth has a structure that resembles the structure of an egg in some ways. The central core is like the yolk of the egg. This is surrounded by the mantle, which is like the white of the egg. And all of it is surrounded by the crust, which is like the shell of the egg.

The deeper we go into the earth, the hotter it gets. By the time we get to the Gutenberg discontinuity, the temperature is about 5000° F. The mantle is solid, but it is very hot.

The core is even hotter.

There are two kinds of body waves. One kind moves forward and backward and is called a *longitudinal wave*. The other moves left and right and is called a *transverse wave*.

32

When a longitudinal wave reaches the Gutenberg discontinuity, it changes direction but keeps on going. A transverse wave, however, stops at the Gutenberg discontinuity and goes no farther.

Scientists knew that a longtitudinal wave can travel through a liquid but a transverse wave cannot.

They concluded, therefore, that earth's core must be liquid since it will not transmit a transverse wave. Since the core is liquid and very dense, it must be metal instead of rock. The most common dense metal is iron, so most scientists think that the earth's core is a mass of liquid iron, together with a small quantity of nickel, an element very similar to iron.

So earthquakes aren't all bad. At least they have given us information about the inside of the earth, right down to the center. It is information we might never have been able to get any other way.

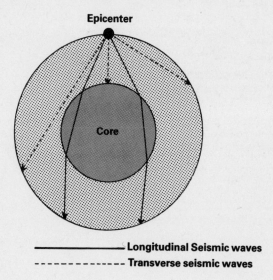

Epicenter

Core

———————————— **Longitudinal Seismic waves**
– – – – – – – – – – – – **Transverse seismic waves**

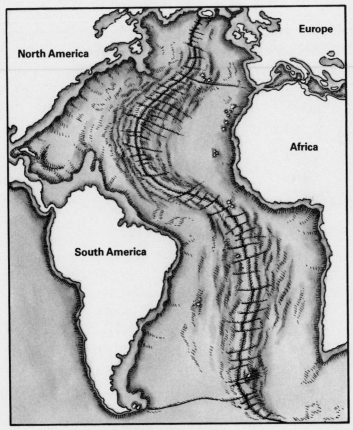

Mid-Atlantic Rift

Methods for measuring the depths of the ocean bottom continued to be improved. A group of American scientists, under William Maurice Ewing (YOO-ing) (1906–1974), made detailed measurements in the 1950s.

In 1953 Ewing announced that there is a deep canyon running down the middle of the Mid-Oceanic Range. It came to be called the *Great Global Rift*.

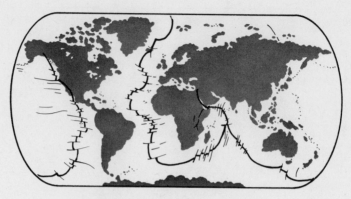

World wide Mid-Oceanic Range

The rift seems to mark off the earth's crust into a number of solid pieces called *plates*. Some of these plates are huge.

Part of the rift runs along the rim of the Pacific Ocean. At the west of the Pacific Ocean it follows the line of islands east of Asia. At the north it follows the line of the Aleutian Islands. On the east it runs along the rim of western North America. In fact, it cuts across the western edge of California. The San Andreas fault is part of the crack that surrounds the Pacific.

The Pacific Plate, then, is under most of the Pacific Ocean. East of the Pacific Plate is the North American Plate, which extends out to the middle of the Atlantic Ocean. South of the North American Plate is the South American Plate, which also extends out to the middle of the Atlantic Ocean.

On the other side of the rift in the middle of the Atlantic Ocean is the Eurasian Plate in the north and the African Plate in the south. These two are sepa-

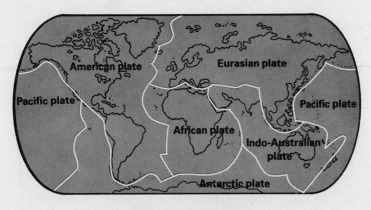

Major tectonic plates

rated by a crack that runs along the Mediterranean Sea and the Persian Gulf. East of the African Plate is the Australian Plate, and to the south is the Antarctic Plate.

In addition to these eight large plates there are smaller ones here and there. An example is the Nazca Plate just west of South America.

Thanks to seismographs, it is possible for scientists to locate all the earthquakes that take place. It turns out that almost all of them are located on the cracks between the plates.

It seems that the plates are moving and rubbing against each other and that is causing the earthquakes.

But why should the plates be moving?

In 1962 the American scientist Harry Hammond Hess (1906–1969) suggested that material from the mantle is moving up to the sea bottom through the Great Global Rift in the middle of the Atlantic Ocean.

It is this material that formed the great mountain

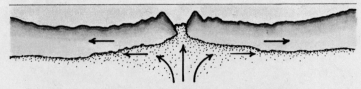

Mantle material rising to separate plates

range running down the middle of the Atlantic Ocean. As this material forces itself upward, it spreads out on the sea floor and makes it wider. That pushes the North American Plate and the Eurasian Plate apart.

North America and Europe *are* drifting apart, as Wegener had said. This is not, however, because the continents are floating. That was Wegener's mistake.

The continents are fixed firmly to the plates, but the plates, with the continents on them, are being forced apart.

This notion of "sea floor spreading" was shown to be correct. Scientists found that the floor of the Atlantic Ocean is much younger than the continents; the closer to the middle, the younger it is.

Well, then, hundreds of millions of years ago Pangaea did exist. Different parts of it were on different plates, however, and there were long faults between the plates.

Material coming up from the mantle gradually spread those faults and pushed portions of Pangaea away from one another, forming sections of ocean in between.

Maybe, hundreds of millions of years from now, all the continents will be pushed together again by the moving plates to form a new Pangaea, and then it will break up again and so on.

The various plates cover the whole earth. This means that if plates are being pushed apart in some places, plates are being forced together in other places. If two plates come together very slowly, they crumple where they meet and form mountain ranges.

Thus, because the Atlantic Ocean is getting wider, the North American Plate pushes against the Pacific Plate, and this pushing has made ranges of mountains along the western shore of North America.

If two plates come together a little faster, one plate slips under the other. The plate that slips under moves slowly into deeper parts of the mantle and melts.

At the places where plates pull apart or push together, volcanoes form, islands are pushed above the ocean surface, and the ocean bottom is pulled down to form *trenches*, which are especially deep parts of the ocean. In fact, a great many things can now be understood about the earth that couldn't be understood before the plates were discovered.

The study of the way in which the earth's crust bends and twists is called *tectonics* (tek-TON-iks). Scientists now talk about *plate tectonics* as the study of the movement of the great plates that make up the crust of the earth.

It is plate tectonics that has finally made it possible to understand why earthquakes take place. There are very slow circular currents of material in the earth's hot mantle, scientists believe, that have probably started because of the earth's rotation. The moving currents drag the plates apart in some places and push them together in other places.

Where the plates are dragged apart, material from the mantle pushes upward. Where the plates are pushed together, there is crumpling, or the crust is forced down into the mantle.

In the places where hot material moves up, or where cold material crumples or moves down, there is movement of rock against rock and earthquakes take place.

Of course, earthquakes don't take place all the time. As plates are pulled apart or forced together, a section of rock on one plate is pushed sideways, upward or downward, against a section of rock on the neighboring plate. Friction holds the rock in place, however.

More and more pressure is placed on the rock, though, until it finally gives. One section of rock slides suddenly against the other and then sticks, then slides again, and so on. Each time it slides, there is an earthquake. The longer it sticks in place between slides, the greater the pressure buildup, the more sudden and sharp the final movement, and the larger the earthquake that results.

6 What Do We Do?

IN THE middle 1970s there was news of a great many earthquakes. On July 27, 1976, there was an earthquake in China that destroyed a whole city south of the Chinese capital, Peking, and killed about 650,000 people. This was the worst earthquake disaster in over four hundred years. There were other bad earthquakes in Guatemala, Mexico, Italy, the Philippines, Romania, and Turkey.

Are things getting worse? Are the earth plates out of control? Are human beings doing something that is upsetting the earth?

Probably not. It is no worse than it has been before. It's just that we notice earthquakes more nowadays.

In the twentieth century we've developed radio and television, so we hear about disasters more quickly. In 1900, if there was an earthquake in a remote part of Asia, people in Europe or North America might not even have heard about it. Nowadays we have a

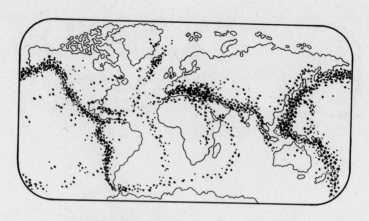

Sites of Major Earthquakes 1900-1966

worldwide network of seismographs that detect a distant earthquake at once and locate it exactly. Then newspaper reporters and television cameras send out the information everywhere.

Also, we have grown more interested in the outside world. In 1900, even if Americans or Europeans heard of an earthquake in a far distant corner of the globe, they wouldn't have cared much. Nowadays, though, many people travel all over the world, and distant places don't seem so distant anymore. An earthquake far away seems important, and we pay more attention.

Finally, the population of the earth is nearly three times as high now as it was in 1900, and many cities have increased in population far more than three times. In 1900, for instance, there were only about one hundred thousand people in Los Angeles; but nowadays there are nearly three million.

Then, too, buildings have become much more elaborate and expensive, and there are more of them. Think of all the factories, dams, power plants, airline terminals, and oil pipelines that now exist. In fact, there are many man-made things now that didn't exist at all at the beginning of the century.

This means that an earthquake of a certain size and in a certain place can kill more people and do much more damage to property now than that same earthquake of the same size and in the same place would have done in 1900.

California earthquake 1971

All these reasons explain why earthquakes seem to have grown so much worse in recent years, even though the earth isn't trembling any more than it used to.

Is there anything we can do to make the danger less?

We could stay away from places where earthquakes are likely. But some of those places are very good to live in otherwise, and people don't want to stay away.

If people must live in earthquake zones, buildings should be designed so that when an earthquake comes they can sway but not collapse. It is the collapse of buildings that does most of the killing. Of course, such designs are expensive.

If there is any way we can predict when an earthquake is about to come, people might at least get out of their houses, or leave an area altogether. Then, even if property is destroyed, at least lives are saved.

How do you predict an earthquake?

Some changes have been reported to take place before an earthquake. The ground might hump upward along a fault, for instance.

Then, too, tiny shakings begin. Rocks begin to pull apart slightly so that water sinks deeper into them. Or water that was imprisoned before leaks out and moves upward.

This means that there are changes in the water level in wells, or an increase in muddiness as sand and soil shake into the water.

Certain gases that are usually imprisoned in rock can now leak out and be detected. There are changes in the way the ground conducts small electrical currents, or changes in the natural magnetism of the rocks.

None of these changes makes it certain that an earthquake will come or, if it does, exactly where the epicenter will be, or how strong it will be, or at what time it will come. Maybe as we learn more and devise better instruments, we can make the predictions more certain.

We might not even need instruments. There are reports that animals become very uneasy just before an earthquake. Horses suddenly begin to rear and race, dogs howl, fish leap. Animals like snakes and rats, which usually remain hidden in holes, suddenly come out into the open. In zoos, chimpanzees become restless and spend more time on the ground.

This isn't because animals have strange senses that human beings don't have. It's that they live closer to nature and pay more attention to small things about them. They can feel tiny tremblings and hear small noises as the rock masses get ready to slide.

In China, where earthquakes are more common and more damaging than in the United States and where the population is larger, the people are encouraged to notice the things about them very carefully. Any strange actions of animals, any strange sounds in the earth, any shifts in the level of well water, even any unusual flaking of paint, are reported.

The trouble is that it is hard to tell when these changes mean an earthquake is coming and when they take place for other reasons.

A horse can suddenly start running just because it's been stung by a bee, there can be a strange noise from the ground just because a rock has tumbled down a mountainside, and so on. On the other hand, some earthquakes can come so suddenly that there is hardly any warning at all.

The Chinese report that they have been able to predict some earthquakes. There was one in northeastern China on February 4, 1975, which was 7.3 on the Richter scale, and it was predicted. People left the area and many lives were saved. On the other hand, the even larger earthquake of July 27, 1976, was *not* predicted, and a whole city was wiped out.

Peking   August 9, 1977

Perhaps it is better not to take chances. As soon as there is *any* sign that an earthquake might come, maybe everyone should leave. If there's no earthquake, they can all go back.

But leaving is very troublesome. People don't want to leave their homes just because there *might* be a quake. Business would be upset, too, and everyone

54

would lose money. And there is always the chance that when most people leave an area, some might remain behind and loot the empty buildings. And trying to evacuate a large city might cause almost as much trouble and expense as a small earthquake.

If people left an area a couple of times, went to a lot of trouble, lost a lot of money, and then found out it was a false alarm, they would be very annoyed. Eventually, when there was a warning, they would probably refuse to budge, and the earthquake might really occur that time.

The thing to do is to work to improve our prediction system. Once we can actually say that an earthquake of a particular strength will strike at a particular place at a particular time, and be almost always proved right, *then* people will leave in a hurry.

What about preventing an earthquake?

There is no way human beings can stop the earth's plates from moving. Nor can they stop masses of rock from rubbing and moving against other masses of rock.

Perhaps, though, we can make it *easier* for the rocks to move. As pressure builds on the rocks, they could slide along a little, then stick, then slide along a little, then stick, then slide along a little, and so on. This could produce a number of small earthquakes every year. Hundreds of such small earthquakes spread over fifty years might shake the dishes or rattle the windows now and then but do no real damage.

Or else the rocks might slide along a little and then stick—and stick, and stick, and stick, and not move at all for fifty years because they stick so hard. The pressure builds up, and then, all at once, the rock slides in a few minutes the distance that might have been spread out over those fifty years. *That* produces a giant earthquake.

Maybe we can encourage the rocks to slip along more easily and produce only the small earthquakes.

Suppose deep wells are drilled along a fault and water is forced into them. The water might find its way between the masses of rock and make them just a little more slippery. That would encourage the small slides, and a giant earthquake would never appear.

Will this work? We don't know.

If it is ever tried and if it does work, or if some other way is found to make the rocks slip gradually, then perhaps we will never again have to live in fear of earthquakes.

Index